Form and Dichroic Light

Form and Dichroic Light

Scott Hall at Carnegie Mellon University

Michelle LaFoe and Isaac Campbell
OFFICE 52 Architecture

Foreword by Cesar Pelli, FAIA
Introduction by Michael J. Crosbie, FAIA

Leete's Island Books, Sedgwick, Maine

Published by
Leete's Island Books
Post Office Box One
Sedgwick, Maine 04676
207.359.5054

Printed in Maine, First Edition

ISBN 9780918172709

Design and Layout: Michelle LaFoe and Isaac Campbell
Cover Design: Michelle LaFoe and Isaac Campbell
Editing and Proofreading: Stuart Campbell
Special thanks: Peter Neill, publisher, Mary Barnes, advisor

Font: Garamond

OFFICE 52 Architecture
Scott Hall at Carnegie Mellon University
www.office-52.com

Image Credits:

Jeremy Bittermann 2, 6-7, 8, 10, 46, 54 (bottom right), 55
(bottom), 57, 59 (bottom), 60-61, 62, 63, 64-65, 66-67,
68-69, 70-71, 72-73, 74, 75, 76, 77, 78, 80, 84, 87, 90-91,
92, 93, 95

Isaac Campbell 15 (all), 20 (top, renderer), 32 (top left,
renderer), 33 (top right, renderer), 37 (renderer), 38-41,
47, 48-49 (top), 50-51, 52 (top, renderer; bottom right,
photography), 53 (bottom), 56 (bottom), 58, 59 (top),
83 (bottom right), 85, 86 (bottom left)

Richard Hoyen 25-27 (renderer)

Dan Kvitka 88-89 (bottom 3 images, photographer)

Michelle LaFoe 16 (renderer sketchbook), 21 (top,
bottom), 22 (bottom, renderer painting), 23 (middle,
bottom), 82 (renderer, sketchbook), 83 (top, renderer),
83 (bottom left), 86 (top, middle, bottom right), 88-89
(renderer, oil pastels), cover (renderer, oil pastels)

OFFICE 52 Architecture studio 18-19, 20 (bottom),
21 (middle), 22 (top), 23 (top), 28-29, 30-31, 32-33 (top
middle, bottom model photography), 34-36, 48-49
(bottom rendering), 52 (bottom left), 53 (top left and
right), 54 (top left and right, bottom left), 55 (top left and
right), 56 (top)

Shaun Selberg 12 (renderer), 42-45 (renderer)

Contents

Foreword

by Cesar Pelli, FAIA

Architecture is a marvelous profession that has the potential to be one of the great arts with the opportunity to create moving relationships with inert materials. Architects can work towards practical yet sublime results, with a depth of emotion provoked by the architecture itself. The creative act is in the process that unfolds in the design studio, where one practices architecture. My first experience with this process was during the ten years I worked with Eero Saarinen, the son of the prominent Finnish architect Eliel Saarinen and textile designer Loja Saarinen. I am grateful to have had the opportunity to pass this lineage along to the many designers who have worked with me in my office.

One of the great joys of teaching is that we are always learning, and one of the greatest pleasures I have had as an educator and practitioner has been to work with younger designers and see them develop into mature, talented and thoughtful architects. Some have moved on to start their own firms, and through their work, they demonstrate a continued exploration of ideas and the fundamental beliefs that shape us, our buildings, and our cities, the principal factors for which I have been looking at for years in my practice.

Isaac Campbell and Michelle LaFoe are two such designers that continue this lineage. Both are graduates of the Rice School of Architecture, and they each made their way to New Haven, Connecticut through different paths and worked with me for a number of years on various design projects. Isaac was talented and industrious and soon demonstrated an ability to lead teams and interface with clients. Michelle, who also has a background in Fine Arts, was an intuitive and creative designer who worked with me to give sculptural form to many projects, one in particular being the complex entry for the National Museum of Contemporary Art in Osaka, Japan.

It was with pleasure that I learned in 2010 that they had opened their own firm, OFFICE 52 Architecture, and that soon thereafter they had won a national competition to design Scott Hall, the new Nano-Bio-Energy Technologies Building at Carnegie Mellon University in Pittsburgh, Pennsylvania. Scott Hall recently opened, and Michelle and Isaac continue the evolution from Saarinen's design process to my own, with a focus on the importance of the physical model to study the form, texture and color of the architecture and the spaces they've created. Within their design, I see a continuity of the formative studio conversations we had in New Haven about the fundamental values and principal factors affecting the art of architecture.

March 2017

Introduction:
The Architecture of the Not So Obvious

by Michael J. Crosbie, FAIA

One definition of genius in architecture is the ability to divine a solution to a particularly demanding design problem that seems so obvious that it presents itself as the very best answer as soon as you see it. The campus of the Haystack Mountain School of Crafts designed by Edward Larabee Barnes in the early 1960s is a case in point. Presented with a heavily wooded, aggressively sloping site on a Maine hillside that disappeared into the Atlantic Ocean, Barnes composed his campus buildings to ride above the land, touching down gently with pier foundations that kept the architecture's impact on the site to an absolute minimum. Here is an obvious solution that is elegant in its approach and reverent to its place. Another tack in architectural problem solving is to reject the conventional wisdom of the most obvious solution and, by a thorough analysis of the given site and project circumstances, bring forth a design that turns the obvious on its head, defying the predictable answer. This is also a mark of design virtuosity and the case of Scott Hall.

As the architects, Isaac Campbell and Michelle LaFoe of OFFICE 52, explain in their detailed recounting in this book about the design process, the conventional wisdom (the best answer as suggested by a pre-existing study) was to stack the building in such a way that nevertheless retained a campus eyesore and would have disrupted existing utility lines. In contrast, OFFICE 52 divined a design solution that melded the two types of solutions described above: not at all obvious and counter to conventional thinking, but once explored and realized presented itself as eminently obvious—the very best answer to the problem. Part of that ingenious answer was to bring the building down on point foundations that accommodated the existing utility lines, similar to the way Barnes did at Haystack, and bury new laboratory spaces most sensitive to vibration into the area of the campus eyesore, making it disappear into firm ground.

The architecture of Eero Saarinen is often cited as reflective of such ingenious design. Saarinen's approach to design was often a trail-blazing conception of the problem that evolved into the most obvious answer once it was conceived and realized. The elegant, single, arching spine of the Ingall's Hockey Rink at Yale University, for example, is a bold architectural gesture—not obvious at all—that immediately appears as the one right solution to covering a large volume in such a way that does not wreak havoc to the scale and texture of its neighborhood context. Dulles International Airport is another instance in which Saarinen questioned the conventional wisdom of airport design and created a new prototype for the contemporary airport in moving passengers from the terminal to the aircraft. Saarinen's architecture has often been described as

View of Scott Hall's North Wing and new bridge

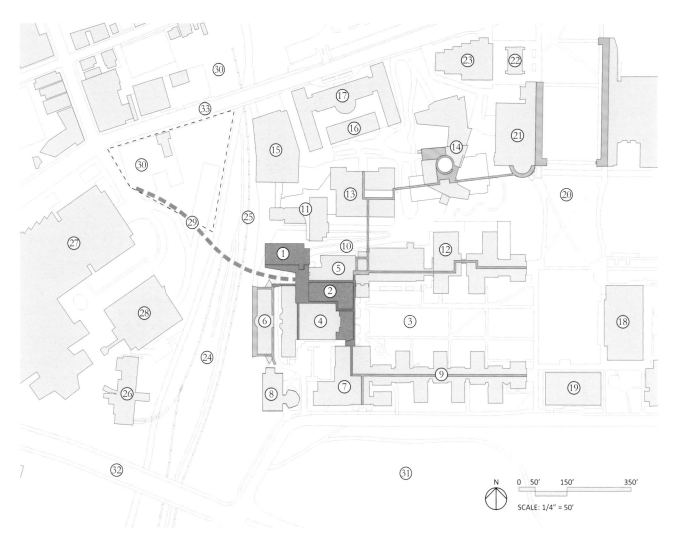

Site and Connections Plan

1. Scott Hall North Wing
2. Scott Hall Bertucci Nanotechnology Lab
3. Hornbostel Mall (open space)
4. Hamerschlag Hall
5. Wean Hall
6. Roberts Hall
7. Porter Hall
8. Scaife Hall
9. Baker Hall
10. Hamerschlag Drive
11. FMS Building
12. Doherty Hall
13. Newell-Simon Hall
14. Gates and Hillman Building
15. Collaborative Innovation Center
16. Smith Hall
17. Hamburg Hall

18. College of Fine Arts
19. Hunt Library
20. The Cut (open space)
21. Purnell Center for the Arts
22. Warner Hall
23. Cyert Hall
24. Junction Hollow (ravine)
25. Active Rail Line
26. Bellefield Plant
27. Carnegie Museum of Art
28. Parking Garage
29. Future Pedestrian Bridge
30. Proposed Future Development
31. Schenley Park
32. Schenley Drive
33. Forbes Avenue

Key

Scott Hall

Existing Buildings

Existing Interior Circulation

New Circulation

N   0 50'   150'   350'

SCALE: 1/4" = 50'

lacking a signature style. Every new commission demanded a fresh approach to the stated design problem, a style that was special to the job, as the architect described it. In Scott Hall, one sees the same willingness on the part of the ... om and obvious answers on their heads, as

d OFFICE 52 might seem considerable
efore the young Portland-based firm was
ne might assume, and the link is found in
d Campbell, Cesar Pelli, who taught them
tectural problem solving while they worked
om Saarinen himself. Pelli and others who
stless genius who was constantly trying to
derstand it in a profound way in an effort
lution to a particular issue and its context.
hitectural "descendants," so to speak, of
52's first major commission, reveals that

that Scott Hall presented for the Carnegie
OFFICE 52 to develop a response that
onceptually framed. Campbell and LaFoe
and developed a plan that diminished and
Hornbostel Mall in front of Hamerschlag
pus, one of CMU's great outdoor rooms,
ed by Henry Hornbostel in the early years
rger context of Pittsburgh's topography,
polis that overlooks the city to the west and
he Hornbostel Mall's energy, which builds
the College of Fine Arts at the east end of
down to Hamerschlag to the west. As one
the acropolis is slowly revealed, while the
hlag begin to obscure the city views as one
cott Hall, the plan opens the view to the
a new outdoor courtyard. As one moves
pace frames the University of Pittsburgh's
of Learning by Charles Klauder, and a
inz Memorial Chapel, just northeast of the
igned by Klauder). This visual and spatial
der spire is significant to the new building's
Bowie Scott were married in the chapel.

The courtyard presents the pedestrian with a number of choices. Moving farther west along ramps and steps interspersed with comfortable, built-in wooden benches, one arrives at a belvedere-like view over Junction Hollow and the city beyond. To the right of the courtyard's terminus, Scott Hall cants slightly to the south, partially containing the space with its visually lush glass façade. What one does not immediately appreciate is that you are standing

on the roof of the new Bertucci Nanotechnology Laboratory built into the loading dock service "pit" previously adjacent to Hamerschlag's north wing. Locating the Bertucci Laboratory here is another stroke of planning genius because it essentially buries the facility into a solid bed of earth that helps to minimize vibrations in the lab spaces. OFFICE 52 announces the presence of the laboratory and celebrates it with a glass pavilion on the south side of the courtyard. This crystalline structure, square in plan and covered with a gently pitched roof with a diagonal ridge, is intimately scaled so as to not compete with Scott Hall directly across the courtyard; their entrances are on axis and face each other.

Entering the glassy pavilion, one circulates down a generous L-shaped staircase that delivers you to the Ruge Atrium on lower level three. Ruge is really the heart of the new complex. It serves as a union point, a knuckle between the four-level Scott Hall to the north and the two-level Bertucci laboratory wing that stretches underneath the mall to the east. Ruge is filled with light and vertical space. During the hour or so I spent sitting in this space, it was a constant hub of meetings, lunches, coffee, and easy chatter. It is free of overt architectural gymnastics. Rather, it is a quiet volume that lets the Carnegie Mellon community of scholars, teachers, researchers, and students to be at ease. Its open staircase allows visitors to scope out who is seated in the atrium, and conversely those relaxing in this space can watch the comings and goings of colleagues and — importantly — potential collaborators. Carnegie Mellon's engineering and science disciplines are noted for their super-collaborative nature, and the Ruge Atrium is just one way that the new building reflects this academic ethic. It is designed as a collaborative-friendly environment, a place of serendipitous encounters where researchers, students, and faculty might meet informally over lunch to discuss a new direction of inquiry or an idea born out of interdisciplinary teamwork.

Scott Hall's sister-space to the Ruge Atrium is the Collaboratory, the moniker for the generous staircases and circulation spaces that stretch along Scott Hall's sun-bathed south wall. You enter Scott Hall's fifth floor from the mall level, and are welcomed into a bright volume whose floors and staircases put the laboratories on display for all to see. Large windows in the labs deliver natural light into these research and learning spaces. The goal of this circulation space is the same as in the Ruge Atrium: to offer opportunities for serendipitous encounters and as welcomed decompression spaces from the high tech/high pressure work in the adjacent labs.

The circulation spaces glow with light generated by Scott Hall's curtain wall, which is a metaphor for the scientific work conducted here. The curtain wall is composed of flat plate glass with vertical and horizontal fins. Elsewhere in this book OFFICE 52 provides a detailed description of how the curtain wall was designed and constructed. Glass layers are a combination of clear and frosted pieces, some with a micro-thin layer of metal oxide (the process echoes the nanotechnology work taking place in the facility). When light passes through these layers it transforms into a range of colors — from warm golds to placid

Site mock-up of curtain wall glass (top), construction images of south elevation, North Wing, morning (middle) and dusk (bottom), p. 15

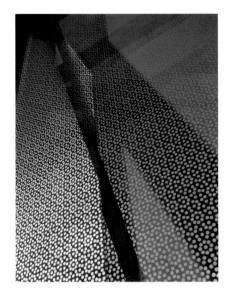

purples — depending on the wavelength of the beam of light. The result is a rainbow of color that changes throughout the day according to the intensity and angle of sunlight striking the glass. Incorporating a color scheme into the design proved rather difficult, as tastes, of course, are mixed. Dichroic glass allows many colors to inhabit these spaces, some for very short periods, others for longer. The light beams move, and at certain times of the year deep and rich pools of color reach far into the building, down a hallway, unfolding across the polished concrete floor. It is an ingenious way to employ ever-changing color into the architecture, and lends the building an aura of luminance.

Another layer of complexity in the curtain wall is the ceramic frit pattern on the glass, which OFFICE 52 designed to be read at a variety of scales: from across the mall and around the north side of Scott Hall, to the intimate scale of a few feet away. The frit design is based on an abstracted photonic nano-pattern of particles that one perceives through atomic microscopes. The silkscreened frit is composed of a dot matrix that shifts as one moves closer to or farther from the glass. The effect can be mesmerizing at close range, and one perceives the shift in scale and the pattern literally transforms before one's eyes. As the pattern moves around the building to the north and east elevations, the frit pattern is read as semitransparent vertical bands contrapuntal to horizontal strips of white brick on a field of gray masonry block. Adding visual depth to the glass envelope, the frit also helps deter birds from flying into the building.

Scientific inquiry is rarely a direct and obvious pursuit. One begins with assumptions, based on past experience. But to push forward one must question hypotheses to uncover blind spots that might obscure pathways to new understandings and conceptual realms. The design of Scott Hall is a product of similar shifts in paradigm. Isaac Campbell and Michelle LaFoe of OFFICE 52 offer us a model for design exploration that focuses like a laser on the nature of the problem, through which one can discover the keys to a solution. It is a way of working and designing that places preeminent value on the responsibility of the architect to keep asking questions, turning over postulations, and carefully following a problem to its vital resolution.

Engage the mind, Inspire the imagination.

Nano - Greek - dwarf - 10^{-9} or one billionth.
If I were one nanometer tall, the earth would be the size of a green pea.

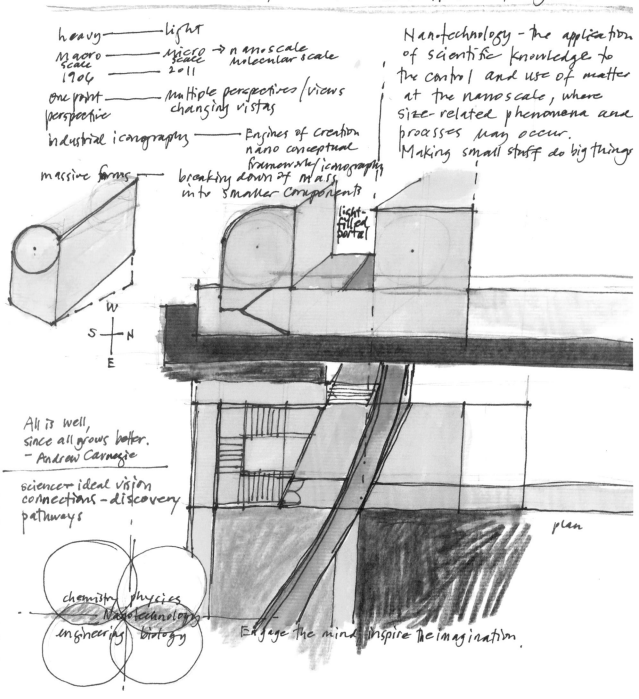

heavy ———— light
Macro ———— micro → nanoscale
scale   scale   molecular scale
1906 ———— 2011
one point ———— multiple perspectives/views
perspective   changing vistas

industrial iconography ———— Engines of creation
                    nano conceptual
                    framework/iconography
massive forms ———— breaking down of mass
                into smaller components

light-filled portal

Nanotechnology - the application
of scientific knowledge to
the control and use of matter
at the nanoscale, where
size- related phenomena and
processes may occur.
Making small stuff do big things

W
S ┼ N
E

All is well,
since all grows better.
- Andrew Carnegie

science←ideal vision
connections - discovery
pathways

chemistry physics
Nanotechnology
engineering biology

plan

Engage the mind, inspire the imagination.

Inversed Forms, Photons and Reverence to Place

by Michelle LaFoe and Isaac Campbell

Carnegie Mellon University has always been known for its groundbreaking research and innovative engineering programs that foster interdisciplinary work in science, art, technology and engineering. When we were asked to participate in an invited national design competition in 2011 for a new nanotechnology, biotechnology and energy technologies building, we were both giddy and apprehensive. Only nine months earlier we had turned the living spaces of our house into a start-up design firm. We would need to match Carnegie Mellon's intensity and quality while being true to our design process and approach, which combine research-based exploration with artistic expression. We had nothing to lose and worked intensely all summer, testing our ideas with study models. The idea we liked best diverged substantially from the written competition parameters, and we thought there was a chance that we could be disqualified. Yet the more we developed our design, the stronger we believed it to be the most compelling solution for the project. The University initially invited seventeen firms to participate in the two-stage design competition and short-listed four for the final interview: OFFICE 52 Architecture, ZGF Architects, Bohlin Cywinski Jackson, and Wilson Architects. Much to our pleasure, we were selected to design the project.

Scott Hall is Carnegie Mellon's newly completed Nano-Bio-Energy Technologies Building for the College of Engineering. The building creates a new research hub for the campus and connects the numerous departments affiliated with the College. The program for the hundred and nine thousand square-foot building includes an eleven thousand square-foot class 10|100 research-grade clean room for exploration at the nano-scale, a new home for the Department of Biomedical Engineering, the Wilton E. Scott Institute for Energy Innovation, the Disruptive Health Technologies Institute, the Engineering Research Accelerator, and a public room composed of the Collaboratory and Ruge Atrium. These initiatives, programs and spaces bring together diverse engineering disciplines and external partnerships for collaboration and exploration in new methods of creative and intellectual inquiry. In essence, Scott Hall is a campus within a campus anchoring the west end of the Hornbostel Mall. Completed in 2017 with a total construction cost of $81.5 million, Scott Hall recently received LEED Gold certification and is one of the most energy efficient lab buildings of its type in the country.

At the outset of the competition, we built a site model to quickly test our ideas with study models constructed by hand and digital fabrication. Our studio's aesthetic approach is to test our ideas in physical models, which to us provides an objective way of looking at architecture. Even though physical models do

Sketchbook excerpt, p. 16
Competition site model, p. 18-19

17

19

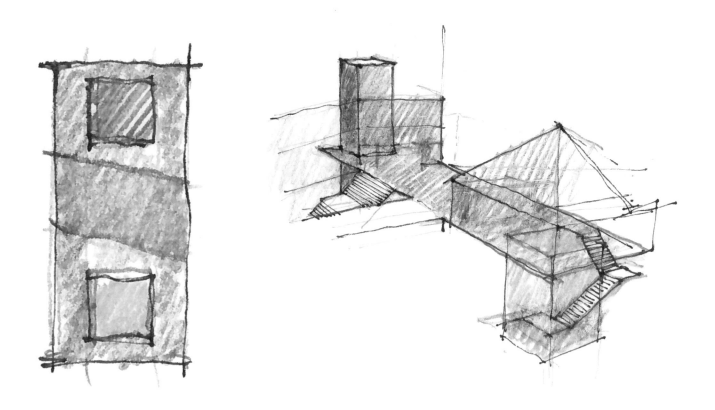

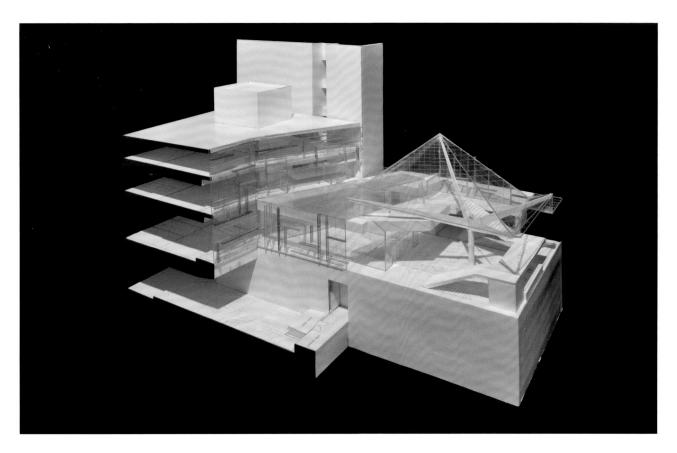

not reveal everything about a design, they are a close approximation to reality. With our projects we also use advanced 3D computer modelling. While this suffices for certain concepts, it cannot replace the efficacy and creativity of the physical study model, which we typically use to test several ideas simultaneously until we arrive at the best solution for the site and program. The physical models are also an efficient way to share ideas with clients, who are intuitively drawn to the tactile qualities and are better able to understand our design and intent, which include the overall vision, functional and artistic objectives, and potential of the project. Concurrently, we write a brief about what we are seeking so that the purpose is articulated and each design has a conceptual backbone. Typically this is adjusted as the design develops, as happened with Scott Hall.

Our approach to the competition began by questioning established preconceptions and the prescribed conceptual planning. Scott Hall is intentionally positioned in the heart of the campus between four existing buildings on an interstitial parcel that drops over 100 feet from the northwest corner of the Hornbostel Mall down into the untamed landscape of Junction Hollow, a neighboring ravine. The lower portion of the site included a steep hillside bisected by an existing service road and major campus utilities. The adjacent ravine is also home to an active freight rail line. The site was so challenging and the building's research program so demanding that we decided a more responsive design approach was required. Early in the competition we spent several days on campus. After returning to the studio and working with our ideas in the physical site model, we developed an architectural vision and proposal that leveraged the project's complex site conditions and intensive research program to transform these challenges into opportunities with an innovative design solution. We decided that building down into Junction Hollow, as the competition brief outlined, was a mistake because the project would have to absorb the cost for relocating major campus utilities in the lower portion of the site. In addition, the freight rail line in the ravine would potentially be a source of vibration and interference for the building's sensitive labs. We instead proposed the relocation of Scott Hall's lower three floors to the top of the site to infill an existing, below-grade service court that unceremoniously terminated the west end of the Hornbostel Mall, one of Carnegie Mellon's prized campus spaces. This outside-the-box thinking differentiated us and our approach from all of our competitors.

The salient design components we proposed that were not in the competition brief included a radically different arrangement of the project's program elements, the expansion of the site boundaries to include underutilized adjacent land, the addition of a public room to the program, use of more natural light, and the design of a contemporary building skin that relates to the proportions and scale of the neighboring buildings and incorporates contemporary scientific concepts. We also created greater physical connectivity through new internal and external pathways that link and integrate the new building into the existing campus on multiple levels. To reinforce this concept, we relocated the project's proposed pedestrian bridge spanning Junction Hollow to begin at Scott Hall's main exterior plaza and to connect to a new diagonal walkway on the building's green roof. This new pathway creates a missing link between the traditional Hornbostel Mall, Scott Hall's exterior walkways and plaza, and the broader campus beyond to future development adjacent to the Carnegie Museum of Art on the other side of the ravine. Physically connecting these spaces strengthens site lines from the mall and Scott Hall and architecturally frames captivating views to the west. The composition and sculptural form of the design ties these elements together with a play on the complex geometry of the site and the varied program components of the building. As a result, the building consists of two interlocking forms — the North Wing, a solid above ground, and the Bertucci Nanotechnology Wing, a below-grade space nestled into a pre-existing void — that embrace at their overlap in a large public room.

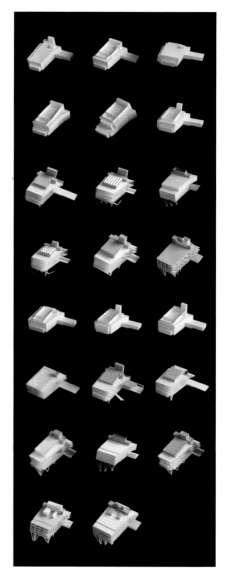

The North Wing projects prominently over Junction Hollow on a composition of sculptural steel columns that gracefully and strategically avoid the major utilities in the hillside below while recalling Pittsburgh's engineering aesthetic. The building's glass form interlocks with a masonry core that joins the building to the hillside. Its transparent skin reveals the activity within and provides occupants with panoramic views of the Carnegie Museum of Art and the city beyond. The building design combines the elegant logic of the traditional Hornbostel Mall and surrounding buildings with our contemporary reinterpretation of their scale, vocabulary, proportions and patterns using modern materials and construction techniques. The North Wing thus has a dual role in the larger composition of the campus. It simultaneously creates a highly visible symbol for the College of Engineering and compositionally reinforces the centrality of Henry Hornbostel's neighboring Hamerschlag Hall, the capstone building at the west end of campus.

To weave the North Wing into the campus lexicon with an appropriate scale, we analyzed the horizontal and vertical proportions of the neighboring buildings to devise a related system for Scott Hall's curtain wall bay dimensions and ceramic frit bands. The scale and density of the frit pattern are derived in part from this study and also respond to specific environmental and solar requirements. Floorplate lines are imperceptible since they are incorporated into the weave of the composition, a conceptual reference to the overlap of disciplines within the building. On a more intimate scale, the curtain wall's ceramic frit draws from the nano-scale science taking place within the building, with the abstraction of a photonic quasi-crystal structure to create a geometric pattern that brings together art, design, technology and science within the architecture. On the south side of the building and along a portion of the west elevation, colorful dichroic glass fins, created with technology commonplace in nano-scale fabrication, shade the building. Their ever-changing reflections and refractions transform the building's appearance depending on the time of day, the intensity of the light, the season, and one's movement in and around the building. Due to their visual depth of color and pattern, the dichroic glass and ceramic frit also help deter birds from flying into the building.

The second interlocking form is an infill building, the Bertucci Nanotechnology Laboratory, which occupies the former sunken service court at the west end

Sketches and competition model 1/4 inch, p. 20
Studio images, p. 21
Massing studies and 20' elevation painting, p. 22
Studio images, p. 23

of the Hornbostel Mall. We relocated the functions of the original service court and placed Scott Hall's most sensitive labs at grade within this space. This significantly improved their desired proximity to other relevant program elements and reduced their exposure to train vibration and other environmental factors. The Bertucci Lab is accessed through a contemporary glass pavilion called the Ruge Atrium. It rises through a state-of-the-art green roof that covers the clean room and extends the traditional landscape of the Hornbostel Mall to the western edge of the historic campus. The Bertucci Lab thus completely transforms this end of the Mall, and it replaces the former service court with contemporary campus spaces, better pedestrian linkages, and ease of connection between buildings above and below grade.

During the competition, we pondered the concept of space for interdisciplinary collaboration and how it can complement the more traditional spaces for contemplative thinking. We decided that there are certain things not easily digitized and replicated online, such as experiences where people interact in a physical space. Space for collaboration should embody a sense of openness and transparency and include places for social interaction to complement virtual connectivity. It should be a place that encourages risk-taking experimentation while providing an environment that fosters connections between disciplines, thereby bringing into contact diverse ways of working.

To that end, we designed the most important public space of the building at the intersection of the North Wing and the Bertucci Lab. We imagined it as a great public room that is the physical and metaphorical center of the building. This space is composed of the Collaboratory and the adjacent Ruge Atrium, which link all four levels of the building and provide direct connections to seven different floor levels in the four neighboring buildings to bring together faculty, researchers, staff and students. In addition, the Collaboratory's four-story space and open public stairway tie together diverse programmatic functions and visually unite the space with vertical and horizontal sightlines that reveal the myriad activities in the building. As the new interactive hub for the College of Engineering, the public room is the intellectual and social heart of the building, providing flexible space for breakout sessions, meetings, exhibits, conferences, and informal social gatherings at the cafe. It is here that all the disciplines of Scott Hall, and those from neighboring buildings, come together and overlap in an environment designed to support interdisciplinary interaction. This public space was not in the original program given by the client, and we were delighted when our idea for it was accepted and built.

Our design for Scott Hall also focused on the physical connectivity and three-dimensional site lines necessary to make this project work on a complex interstitial site. Views and vistas simultaneously extend along major corridors and out to the campus, emphasizing the connectivity of interior and exterior space. Extensive interior glazing offers views into learning, conference and lab spaces with the intent of highlighting the collaborative and interdisciplinary processes happening in the building. The emphasis on transparency also extends to the building's exterior curtain wall, which is articulated with custom-designed ceramic frit and dichroic glass fins for a playful rhythm of color and pattern and providing an abundance of natural light. Scott Hall is thus designed with the intent of creating a sense of openness and possibility, reaffirming the college's mission to foster connections across disciplines while leveraging the constant activity of the public room to energize the building. It is connectivity and illumination on all levels: the visual, architectural and intellectual.

During the design and realization of Scott Hall, we worked with senior leadership from the College of Engineering and Campus Design and Facility Development. They were truly committed and challenged us, as we engaged and challenged them, to think about the overall purpose of the project. They were outspoken and thoughtful, and together we have designed a building that redefines space for interdisciplinary research unique to Carnegie Mellon and creates a new center for the College of Engineering. Scott Hall serves as an experimental platform for creating and presenting works in all engineering disciplines, a flexible research space to encourage new modes of exploration, and a forum for creative partnerships with visiting national and international partners. It is a place that supports cross-disciplinary endeavors, while also recognizing the need for individual contemplation, with the belief that interdisciplinary work will bring about the innovation and dialogue necessary to address global challenges in the twenty-first century. Scott Hall is a testament to the College of Engineering's forward-looking ambitions, and it has ushered in a new architectural paradigm on campus by responding to the pedagogical aspirations of its residents to support traditional and new forms of research, teaching, and interdisciplinary collaboration.

Site Model (pre-existing conditions)

1. Site (red)
2. Hornbostel Mall (open space)
3. Campus utilities
4. Junction Hollow (ravine)
5. Active Rail Line
6. Hamerschlag Drive
7. Hamerschlag Hall
8. Wean Hall
9. Roberts Hall
10. Scaife Hall
11. Porter Hall
12. FMS Building
13. Newell-Simon Hall
14. Baker Hall

Site Model (with Scott Hall)

1. Scott Hall - North Wing
2. Scott Hall - Bertucci Nanotechnology Lab
3. Green Roof - Mall Extension
4. Ruge Atrium Entry

5. Entry Plaza
6. Future Pedestrian Bridge
7. Hamerschlag Plaza
8. Porter Hall Entry Pavilion

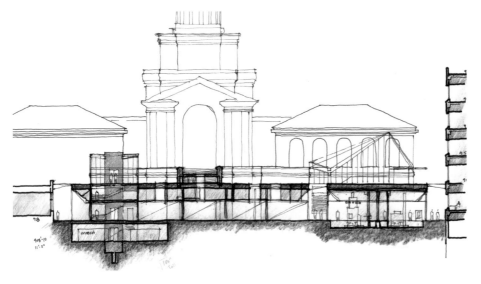

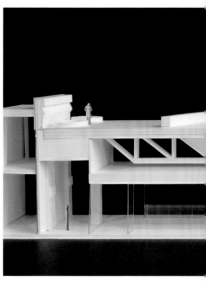

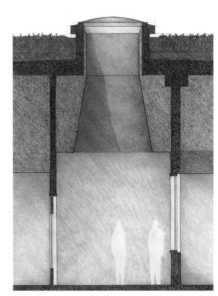

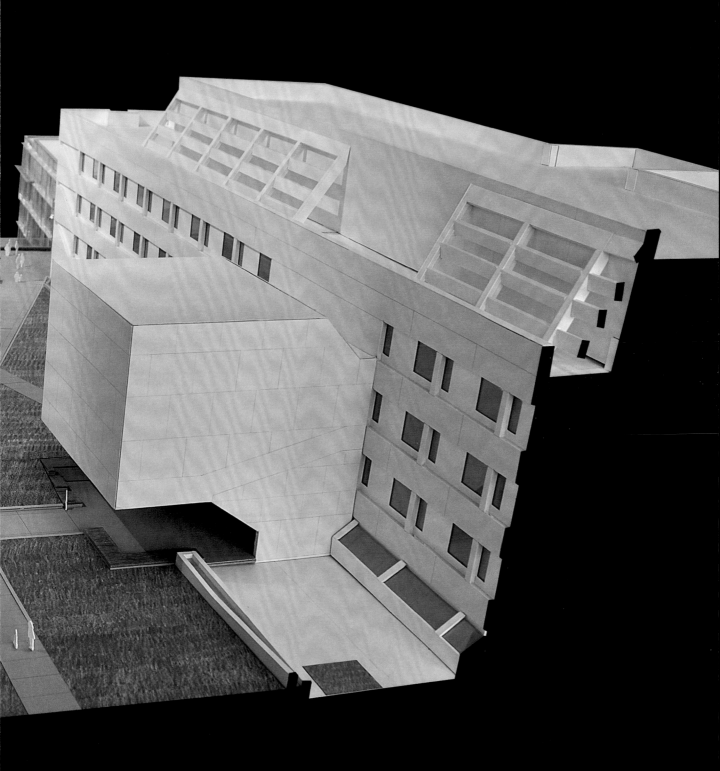

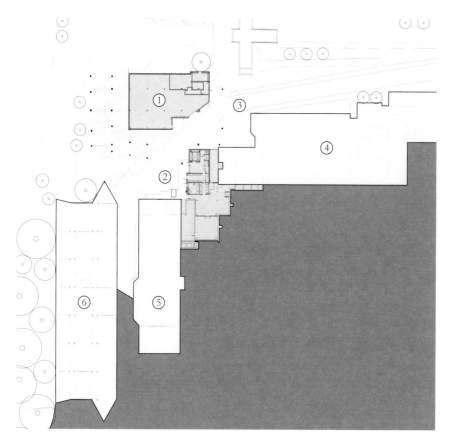

Level Two Plan

1. Mechanical room
2. Loading docks
3. Existing Hamerschlag Drive
4. Existing Wean Hall
5. Existing Hamerschlag Hall
6. Existing Roberts Hall

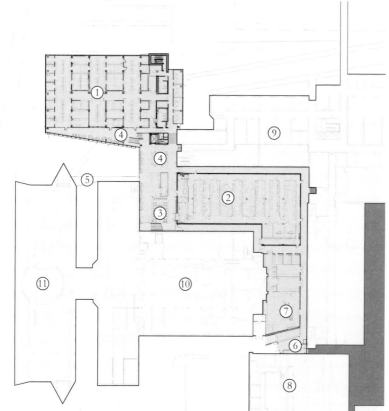

Level Three Plan

1. Biomedical Engineering Labs
2. Bertucci Nanotechnology Lab and support
3. Ruge Atrium and cafe
4. Collaboratory
5. New Bridge to Roberts Hall
6. Porter Hall Entry Pavilion
7. South Mechanical Room
8. Existing Porter Hall
9. Existing Wean Hall
10. Existing Hamerschlag Hall
11. Existing Roberts Hall

Level Four Plan

1. Biomedical Engineering Departmental Center
2. Collaboratory
3. Ruge Atrium
4. Bertucci Nanotechnology Lab support
5. South Mechanical Room
6. Porter Hall Entry Pavilion
7. Existing Porter Hall
8. Existing Wean Hall
9. Existing Hamerschlag Hall
10. Existing Roberts Hall

Level Five Plan

1. Wilton E. Scott Institute for Energy Innovation
2. Collaboratory
3. Scott Hall Entry Plaza
4. Ruge Atrium Entry
5. Bertucci Nanotechnology Lab Greenroof
6. Hamerschlag Plaza
7. Porter Hall Entry Pavilion
8. Scott Hall Skylight
9. Existing Porter Hall
10. Existing Wean Hall
11. Existing Hamerschlag Hall
12. Existing Roberts Hall

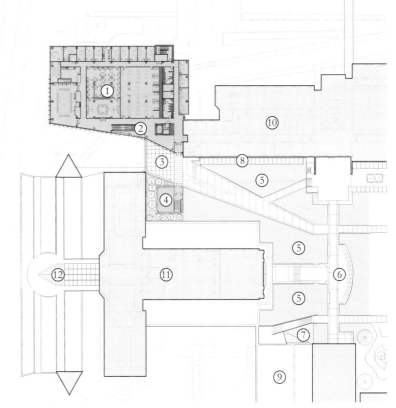

43

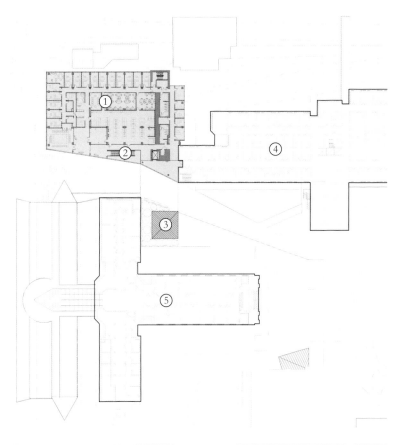

Level Six Plan

1. Institute for Disruptive Health Technologies and the Engineering Research Accelerator
2. Collaboratory
3. Ruge Atrium
4. Existing Wean Hall
5. Existing Hamerschlag Hall

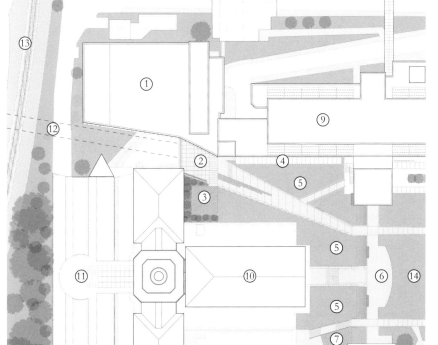

Site Plan

1. Scott Hall North Wing
2. Scott Hall Entry Plaza
3. Ruge Atrium Entry
4. Scott Hall Skylight
5. Bertucci Nano Lab Green Roof
6. Hamershlag Plaza
7. Porter Hall Entry Pavilion
8. Existing Porter Hall
9. Existing Wean Hall
10. Existing Hamerschlag Hall
11. Existing Roberts Hall
12. Future Pedestrian Bridge
13. Junction Hollow
14. Hornbostel Mall

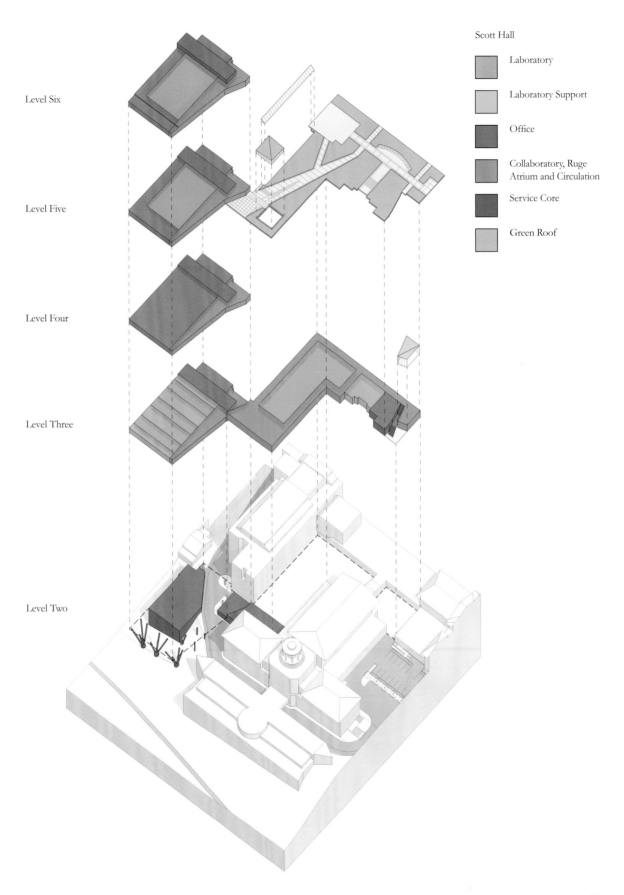

Level Six

Level Five

Level Four

Level Three

Level Two

Scott Hall

Laboratory

Laboratory Support

Office

Collaboratory, Ruge
Atrium and Circulation

Service Core

Green Roof

Points of Construction

by Michelle LaFoe and Isaac Campbell

Twenty-three of the structural steel columns that support the North Wing visibly connect to its soffit in a regularized grid. These columns are located on the west and south sides of the building, and they slope to meet the ground in three pod formations. Immediately below these are strategically placed concrete pier foundations in the hillside that avoid the primary campus utilities, which remained in place and were not subject to costly relocation. In addition, the building spans Hamerschlag Drive, an existing road that bisects the site. The building's columnar support system and pier foundations were designed so that their placement would have minimal impact on the existing site conditions and major utilities, including the university's primary electrical feed, buried in the steep hillside.

Three existing buildings define the irregularly shaped interstitial space — or void — previously a sunken service court, into which the Ruge Atrium and Bertucci Nanotechnology Lab are constructed. This part of Scott Hall is built below grade. To mitigate vibration, the lab space is built with a heavy concrete frame with a fourteen-inch thick roof slab, two-foot square columns, and an eighteen-inch mat slab foundation set upon existing Bluestone, a type of hard shale. The nanoscience labs and support were placed here so they would not be divided between two floor plates as specified in the original competition brief. Inside the Ruge Atrium and Bertucci Lab area, the original brick and concrete walls of the adjacent buildings are exposed to weave together the existing and the new. A state-of-the-art green roof sits atop this part of the building and creates a seamless extension of the Hornbostel Mall while also revealing itself as a roof, with skylights and two glass entry pavilions at either end of the site.

The geometric form of the North Wing itself is constructed of three-hundred-fifty-four custom unitized curtain wall panels. These panels, which included the insulated glass unit with integral ceramic frit, were prefabricated off-site and installed in only six weeks. Since the building is located on a steep and tight interstitial site, the unitized curtain wall panels were installed from inside the building using techniques developed for high-rise construction. This defined a tectonic more direct and far more efficient and economical than using the standard construction technique of a crane and exterior scaffolding. For the curtain wall system, each unitized panel was precisely placed, allowing the custom designed frit pattern to be read as a unified composition wrapping around the building. Embedded in the curtain wall are stainless steel clips that support the horizontal and vertical dichroic glass fins. They were the last elements installed, and we watched with delight as the photonic transformation began to take effect. Inside the building, the white walls and polished concrete floor reflect the color and light emanating from the dichroic fins, at times bouncing it back to its source.

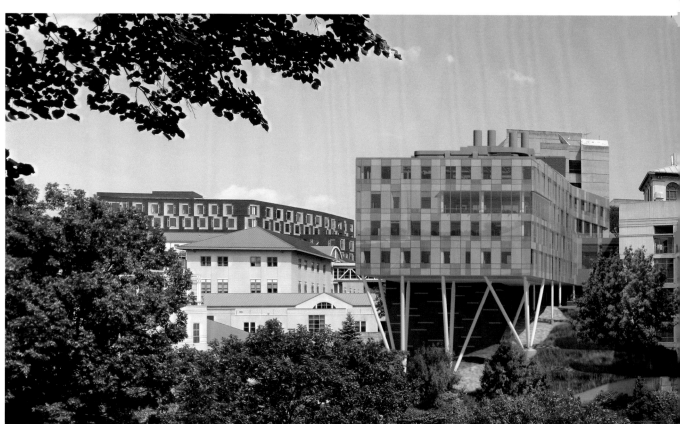

Construction images, North Wing, p. 50-51

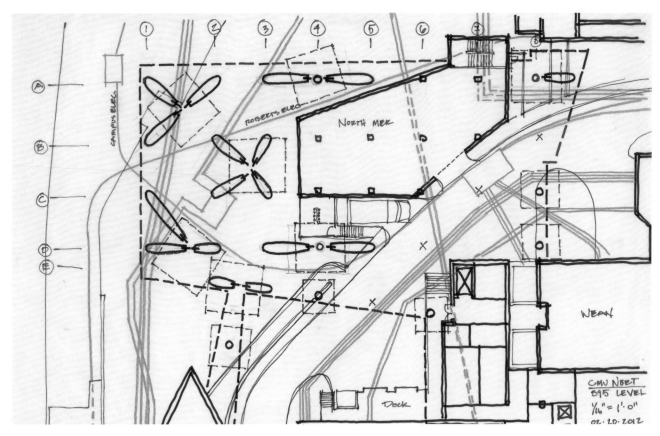

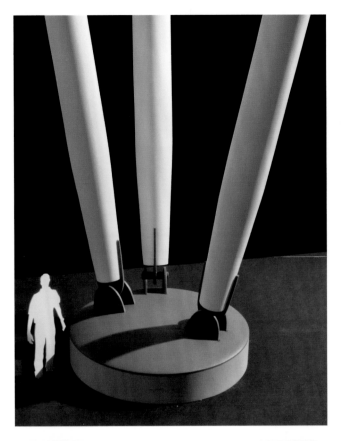

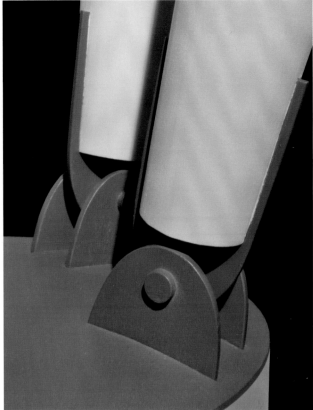

Utility and foundation sketch (top), study model and
   construction image (bottom), p. 52
Column study model (top), construction images (bottom), p. 53

Porter entry study models and view of completed building, p. 54
Ruge Atrium entry study models and view of completed building, p. 55
Model image (top) and construction view (bottom), p. 56
View of Scott Hall's North Wing, morning, p. 57

Pre-existing sunken service courtyard June, 2011 (top), p. 58

Construction of Nanotechnology Lab and Ruge Atrium February, 2015 (middle), p. 58

Completed green roof June, 2016 (bottom), p. 58

Hornbostel Mall before construction June, 2011 (top), p. 59

Horbostel Mall after construction in orange September, 2016 (bottom), p. 59

CLAIRE AND JOHN BERTUCCI
NANOTECHNOLOGY
LABORATORY

Collaboratory and Ruge Atrium, p. 74-75
Collaboratory and bench labs, p. 76
Offices and Bertucci Nanotechnology Lab, p. 77

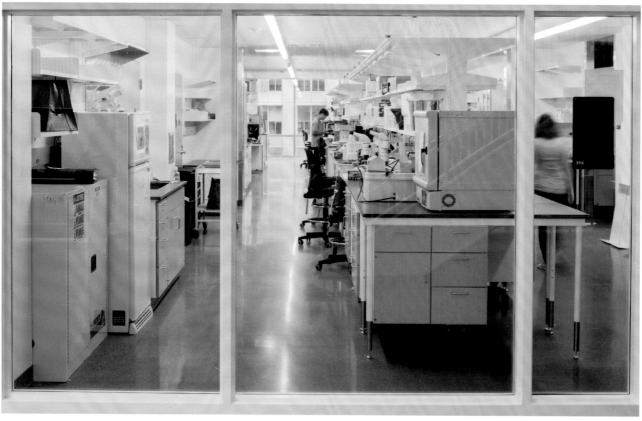

Ephemeral Light and
Evocative Patterns

by Michelle LaFoe and Isaac Campbell

The College of Engineering at Carnegie Mellon University is one of the premier research institutions at the forefront of advanced nanotechnology and complex engineered systems. For Scott Hall's curtain wall design, we focused in part on the innovative research of the college's interdisciplinary programs. This gave us the opportunity to artistically reference the science and technology taking place within the building while metaphorically linking the concepts of nanoscience, scale, photons and light. Leveraging the inherently transformative qualities of dichroic glass and ceramic frit with innovative glass fabrication techniques and a play on scale, we pushed the conceptual limits of glass as a material in the curtain wall to activate the building's interior and exterior spaces. As such, we worked to create an evocative world of constantly changing color, texture and light, the perception of which shifts with the sun's angle and intensity as well as the observer's position in the space.

From the beginning of the project, we were fascinated with the concept of scale in nanotechnology. Nano (from the Greek word *nanos*, meaning dwarf) is a prefix in the SI measurement system (nanometer) that means ten to the negative ninth, or one billionth. Just as with volumetric space, it is about an understanding of scale. During the design process, we looked at the color, materiality, technical capabilities and the light-transmitting qualities of the glass. Our design plays upon the concepts of scale and light in science with the use of dichroic technology for the sun-shading fins, ceramic frit in the curtain wall, and the color of the solar spectrum (wavelength measured in nm). We built in-house mock-ups with dichroic glass in conjunction with computer simulations of the movement of the sun to study the color variations, nano-patterns and sun-shading capabilities of the curtain wall as the solar angle changes.

Dichroic glass has a transmitted color that is completely different from the reflected color because only certain wavelengths of light pass through the metal oxides vaporized onto the glass surface in multiple layers during fabrication. The dichroic float glass is produced in a dip-coating process whereby each layer of metal oxide coating is applied in a thickness of less than one hundred nanometers. The resulting material is about thirty millionths of an inch thick. The manufacturing process is a nanoscience derivative of thin film deposition technology originally developed by NASA in the 1950s and currently used in a multitude of industries such as optics and semiconductors. Due to the advancement of fabrication processes for monolithic architectural applications, glass companies can produce vibrantly transparent dichroic glass for larger scale use, an example being Scott Hall.

During the design process, we looked at a variety of artists and their work in color and light while concurrently researching the concept of nanoscience and dichroic

glass fabrication processes. Source examples we studied include the Lycurgus cup, a fourth century Roman piece made of translucent glass containing colloidal gold and silver particles proportionately dispersed in the glass matrix with changes in color dependent on the location of the light source. We also visited Chagall's thirty-six colored glass installation, entitled *America Window*, on which he drew with metallic oxide paints permanently fused to the glass with heat. For Scott Hall, the compositional placement of the dichroic glass fins in relation to the design of the ceramic frit was of utmost importance in the façade design. We completed numerous sketch studies, paintings and models that weaved the two systems so that they read as one artistic composition.

Ceramic glass frit is analogous to a ceramic glaze for glass and is comprised of minute glass particles, pigment and a medium. Applied by silkscreen print, digital printer or roller to the uncoated monolithic glass, the frit is then fused with heat to the glass. Placed on the number two surface of the insulated glass unit, it acts a sun-shading device and mitigates glare and heat gain. The fabrication process represents a union of modern technology and the craft of traditional printmaking techniques. For color, we completed a comprehensive study of available ceramic glass frit to achieve a subtle light grey that complements the glass and spandrel in the curtain wall. We then chose a dot pattern for the frit to enhance the visual abstraction of the scientific data into a simplified geometry. After completing a sketchbook study of nanotechnology concepts and abstracting them into printable geometries, we built laser-cut mock-ups in Portland and Pittsburgh and worked with the University to choose one that could be universally applied on the curtain wall. On site in Pittsburgh, the construction team built a full-scale mock-up of a bay of the dichroic glass fin and ceramic frit system to confirm the fabrication details of our design aesthetic.

Our custom design of the ceramic frit for the curtain wall at Scott Hall is an abstract geometric representation of a mathematical and microscopic nanoscience structure based on photonic quasicrystals, which influences optical transmission and reflectivity. As such, the design for the frit pattern explores concepts of light and scale, the perception of which changes with one's position. When close-up to the curtain wall glass, one sees a different geometric pattern than when at a greater distance. This is because the ceramic frit was applied in a dot pattern, and the perceived change in scale of our photonic pattern has a similarity to nanoscale particles and quantum physics whereby materials and their particles look and behave differently at different scales. Thus, up-close the pedestrian sees the individual circles and resultant geometric forms that compose the abstracted photonic nano-pattern. Further away, at the scale of the automobile or as passersby on the nearby bridge, the design is read as semi-transparent fields of horizontal and vertical bands of two densities. The dimensions of the bands change as one moves from the south to the north elevation, and their dimensions and proportions relate to the vertical and horizontal compositional elements of the adjacent buildings that surround Hornbostel Mall, and the environmental factors affecting each elevation.

Scott Hall, North Wing curtain wall

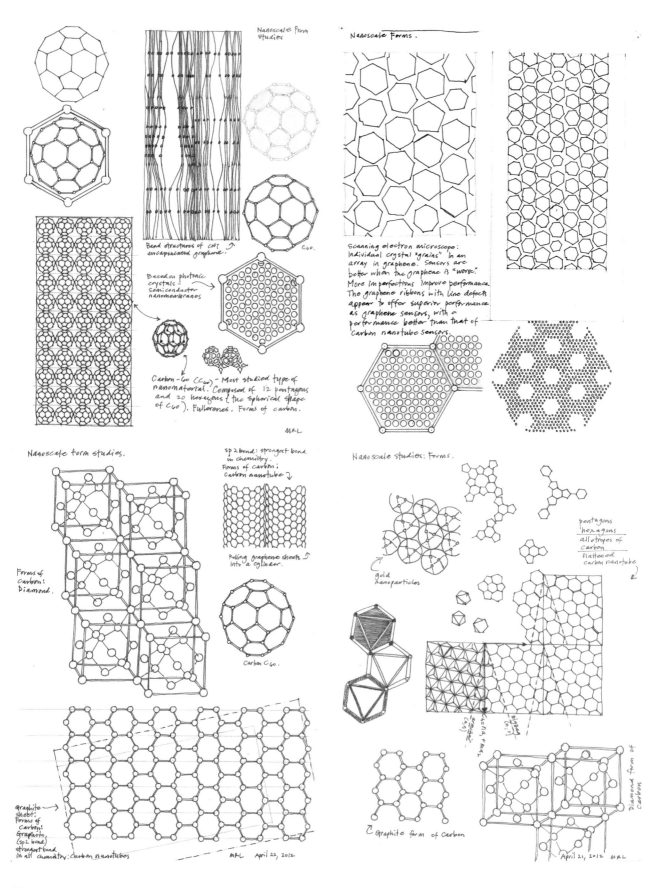

Nanoscale Form studies

Nanoscale Forms.

Band structures of CNT encapsulated graphene.

C_{60}.

Based on photonic crystals: Semiconductor nanomembranes

Carbon-60 (C_{60}) - Most studied type of nanomaterial. Composed of 12 pentagons and 20 hexagons (the spherical shape of C_{60}). Fullerenes. Forms of carbon.

MRL

Scanning electron microscope: Individual crystal "grains" in an array in graphene. Sensors are better when the graphene is "worse." More imperfections improve performance. The graphene ribbons with line defects appear to offer superior performance as graphene sensors, with a performance better than that of carbon nanotube sensors.

Nanoscale form studies.

sp^2 bond: strongest bond in chemistry. Forms of carbon: Carbon nanotube

Rolling graphene sheets into a cylinder.

Forms of Carbon: Diamond.

Carbon C_{60}.

Graphite sheet. Forms of Carbon: Graphite. (sp^2 bond) strongest bond in all chemistry: Carbon nanotubes

MRL   April 22, 2012

Nanoscale studies: Forms.

gold nanoparticles

pentagons hexagons allotropes of carbon flattened carbon nanotube

Graphite form of Carbon

Diamond form of Carbon

April 21, 2012   MRL

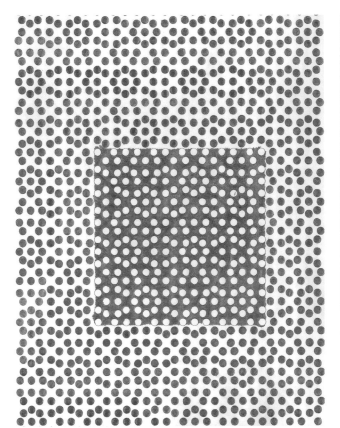

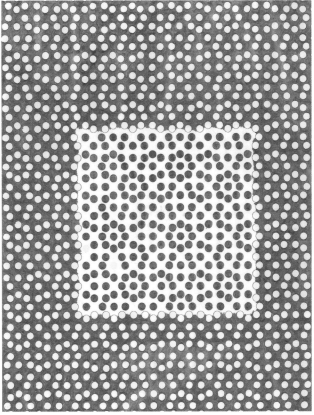

Sketchbook studies of nano structures, p. 82
Abstraction of a photonic quasicrystal structure into ceramic frit pattern, p. 83
Images of curtain wall details, p. 84-85
Light studies in the studio and view of North Wing curtain wall, p. 86-87

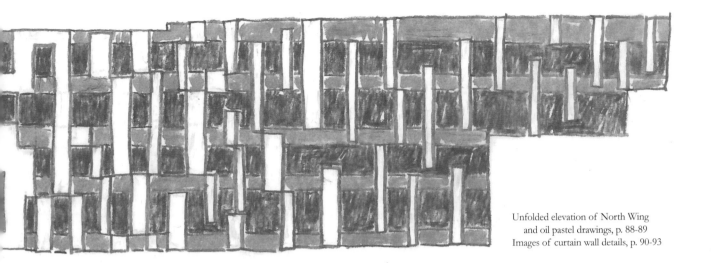

Unfolded elevation of North Wing
and oil pastel drawings, p. 88-89
Images of curtain wall details, p. 90-93

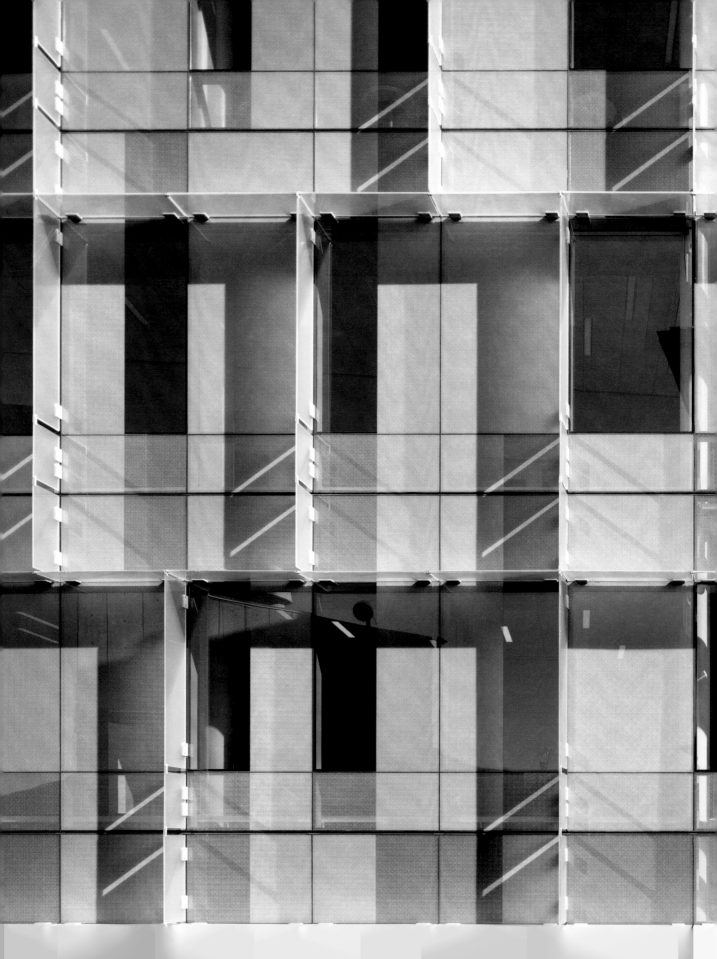

Biographies

Michelle LaFoe, AIA, is a licensed architect and accomplished artist, and as such she has forged a path in both project-based and series-based work. She has designed award-winning higher education, museum and architectural installation projects, and her professional accolades include a Fulbright-Hayes Scholarship and a grant from the Graham Foundation for Advanced Studies in the Fine Arts. She has taught in Rome and Perugia, Italy, lectured at and chaired national conferences, and has exhibited internationally. Michelle earned a Bachelor of Architecture and a Bachelor of Arts at Rice University and a Post-Baccalaureate Graduate degree in Drawing and Painting from the School of the Art Institute in Chicago. As a Distinguished University Research Fellow, she completed her Master of Architecture degree in architectural history and theory and worked with Dr. Richard Betts at the University of Illinois in Champaign-Urbana. Afterwards she completed a year of independent post-graduate research at Yale University in design and fabrication technology. In addition to founding OFFICE 52 Architecture, Michelle has practiced with AIA Gold Medal winner Cesar Pelli, FAIA, at Cesar Pelli & Associates (now Pelli Clarke Pelli Architects) and with Centerbrook Architects.

Isaac Campbell, AIA, is a founding Principal of OFFICE 52 Architecture. For over 25 years, he has planned, programmed and designed highly sustainable environments and award-winning buildings for educational institutions, corporate and private clients in the United States and abroad. His design work has been recognized with awards from both the American Institute of Architects and the Society for College and University Planning. Isaac began his career in the office and AIA Gold Medal winner Cesar Pelli, FAIA, where he quickly became a Design Team Leader for major projects including the Chubu Teiju Cultural Center and Museum in Kurayoshi, Japan and the New York Times Headquarters Competition in New York City. For the last 15 years, much of Isaac's work has focused on creating transformational environments for educational institutions. These include Scott Hall, Carnegie Mellon University's new Nano-Bio-Energy Technologies Building, Tykeson Hall for the College of Arts and Sciences at the University of Oregon, Stanford University's award-winning Science and Engineering Quad, and the new nine-building Knight Management Center for the Stanford's Graduate School of Business. Isaac received his Bachelor of Arts and Bachelor of Architecture from Rice University. He has lectured extensively and has been a guest critic at numerous architecture and design programs across the country.

Cesar Pelli, FAIA, founded the Cesar Pelli & Associates (now Pelli Clarke Pelli Architects) in 1977, the year he became dean of the Yale University School of Architecture. He has designed buildings around the globe, and his work has won numerous awards internationally. In 1995, the American Institute of Architects bestowed upon Pelli the AIA Gold Medal -- the Institute's highest honor. Pelli has written extensively on architectural issues, authoring the book *Observations for Young Architects* in 1999, and has lectured at architecture schools, professional and public gatherings, and at symposia around the world.

Michael J. Crosbie, Ph.D., FAIA, is Professor of Architecture at the University of Hartford, as well as the former Associate Dean and former architecture department chair. He has served as an editor at *Architecture: The AIA Journal,* and *Progressive Architecture,* and is also a frequent contributor to *Oculus* magazine and *Architectural Record*. He is the editor-in-chief of *Faith & Form: The Interfaith Journal on Religion, Art, and Architecture*. Dr. Crosbie is the author of more than 20 books on architecture, and has edited and contributed to approximately 20 others. The author of hundreds of articles on architecture, design, and practice, Dr. Crosbie is a frequent contributor to international print and online publications, and has lectured on architecture throughout the United States and abroad. He is a registered architect and has practiced with Centerbrook Architects and Steven Winter Associates.

Design Credits

Design Architect
OFFICE 52 Architecture
    Isaac Campbell, Principal
    Michelle LaFoe, Principal
    Design Team: Guannan Chen, Cait Coffey, Shaun
    Selberg, Blake Thomas, Jenny Kubo, Jill Asselineau,
    Jeff Tummelson, Sina Meier, Christina Cwiecienski,
    Matt Niebur

Architect of Record
Stantec

Landscape Architect and Civil Engineer
Stantec

Structural Engineer
Arup

Mechanical Engineer
Arup

Electrical Engineer
Arup

Plumbing and Fire Protection Design
Arup

Acoustical and Vibration Consulting
Arup

Lighting Design
Arup

Laboratory Planning
Jacobs Consultancy

Clean Room Design
Jacobs Engineering

Cost Consultant
Davis Langdon

LEED Consultant
evolveEA

Construction Manager and General Contractor
Jendoco Construction Corporation

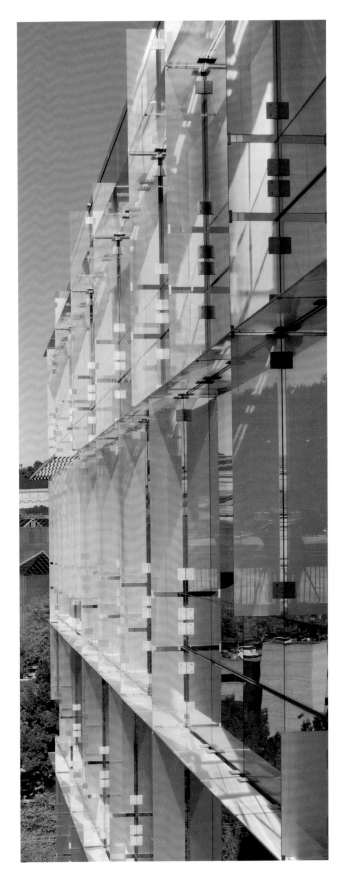

Acknowledgements

We would like to thank Cesar Pelli, Michael J. Crosbie, Jeremy Bittermann and Stuart Campbell, all of whom supported this publication with their contributions and expertise. We would like to give special thanks to Peter Neill, who embraced this book project and challenged us each step of the way with his insights and words of wisdom.

We would like to thank the OFFICE 52 design team and the consultant and construction teams for their commitment in bringing Scott Hall to fruition. In particular we would like to thank: Jill Swensen, Michael Reagan, David Alessi, Kristin Olgaard, Chuck Parker, Alicia Wolfe, Glenn Miller, Emily Putas, Ray Quinn, Jeffrey Huang, Daniel Brodkin, Matt Larson, Carl Mister, George Donegan, Jeff Tubbs, Chris Rush, Joe Solway, Roberto Saldarriaga, Vincent Fiorenza, Tom Grimard, David Mateer, Greg Owen, Bob Patterson, Michael Kuhn, Brian Miller, Ken Brace, Katy Andaloro and Brennen Garrison.

We would like to thank the following members of the Carnegie Mellon community, whose commitment and devoted efforts helped make this project a reality.

Administration

Dr. James H. Garrett Jr., Dean of Engineering
Dr. Pradeep Khosla, former Dean of Engineering
Romayne Botti, Chief Financial Officer, College of Engineering
Dr. Gary Fedder, Professor of Electrical and Computer Engineering, and Vice Provost for Research
Dr. Jared Cohon, President Emeritus and Professor of Civil and Environmental Engineering, former Director of the Wilton E. Scott Institute for Energy Innovation
Dr. Subra Suresh, former President of Carnegie Mellon University
Dr. Mark Kamlett, Professor of Economics and Public Policy and former Provost

Campus Design and Facility Development

Ralph Horgan, Associate Vice President
Bob Reppe, Director of Design
Andrew Reilly, Director of Construction
Ellen Romagni, Director of Business Operations
Max Dorosa, Principal Project Manager
Jennifer McDowell, Principal Project Manager
Karen Spells, Program Coordinator

Faculty and Program

Dr. Yu-li Wang Professor and Department Chair, Biomedical Engineering
Dr. Adam Feinberg, Professor of Material Science and Biomedical Engineering
Dr. Andrew Gellman, Professor of Chemical Engineering and Co-Director for the Wilton E. Scott Institute for Energy Innovation
Dr. Alan Russell, Highmark Distinguished Career Professor, Director of the Disruptive Health Technologies Institute
Matthew Moneck, Clean Room Executive Manager
Chris Bowman, former Clean Room Executive Manager
Gianluca Piazza, Clean Room Faculty Director

Additional gratitude to Martin Altschul, Don Carter, Don Coffelt, Tod Hunt, Steve Lee, Vivian Loftness and Michael Murphy for their wise counsel.

Leadership

We would also like to express our gratitude to the Carnegie Mellon University Board of Trustees, Sherman and Joyce Bowie Scott, Claire and John Bertucci and all of the other donors for their generous support of this building.